	DATE DUE		

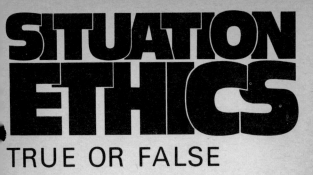

SITUATION ETHICS
TRUE OR FALSE

A dialogue
between
Joseph Fletcher and
John Warwick Montgomery

DIMENSION BOOKS
Bethany Fellowsh[...]
Minneapolis, Minn[...]

0-87123-525-0

DIMENSION BOOKS
Are published by
BETHANY FELLOWSHIP, INC.
6820 Auto Club Road
Minneapolis, Minnesota 55438

Printed in the
United States of America

INTRODUCTION

This book is the transcript of a public dialogue between Prof. Joseph Fletcher and Dr. John Warwick Montgomery at San Diego State College on February 11, 1971. The dialogue was the third event in the San Diego State College's Cultural Arts Board 1970-71 series "Religion and Contemporary Society." Dr. Jack McClurg of S.D.S.C.'s Departments of Philosophy and Religious Studies served as moderator for the discussion. The publishers join with the Cultural Arts Board in hoping that this transcript will give wider circulation to an electric exchange on a subject of vital importance—an exchange which held an audience of 1600 captivated and maximally involved.

Dr. Montgomery's opening statement was read from a prepared text while Professor Fletcher's statement was given ad libitum.

The publishers assume responsibility for the footnotes. They are, of course, not part of the original dialogue but will prove helpful to many readers in clarifying certain items referred to in the course of a lively debate.

THE PARTICIPANTS

Joseph Fletcher

Joseph Fletcher is currently Visiting Professor of Medical Ethics, University of Virginia and Robert Treat Paine Professor, emeritus, Episcopal Theological School (affiliated with Harvard University). He received his A.B. from West Virginia University in 1925, his B.D. from Berkeley Divinity School in 1929, and the honorary degree of S.T.D. from Kenyon College in 1939. He is the author of numerous articles and nine books, the best known of which are *Situation Ethics* and *Moral Responsibility*.

John Warwick Montgomery

John Warwick Montgomery is professor and chairman of the Division of Church History and History of Christian Thought at Trinity Evangelical Divinity School in Deerfield, Illinois, and director of its European program at the University of Strasbourg, France. He holds seven earned degrees including the Doctor of Philosophy from the University of Chicago and the Doctorate of the University in Protestant Theology from the University of Strasbourg, France. He has been regular visiting professor of Theology at Concordia Seminary, Springfield, Illinois, and at De Paul University, Chicago. In 1970 he served as honorary fellow of Revelle College, University of California at San Diego. Among his eighteen books are *The Suicide of Christian Theology, Where Is History Going?,* and *Damned Through the Church.*

Jack McClurg

Jack McClurg is presently associated with the Departments of Philosophy and Religious Studies at San Diego State College. He received his M.D. degree from the State University of Iowa and M.A. and Ph.D. degrees from the University of Chicago. Prior to his appointment at San Diego State College, he taught for ten years in the Biology Department of the University of Chicago.

SITUATION ETHICS

SITUATION ETHICS: TRUE OR FALSE

McCLURG: The question to be debated this evening is situation ethics, true or false. Taking part in the debate are Professor Joseph Fletcher, seated over here, and Dr. John Warwick Montgomery. Dr. Montgomery is over here on my right. Professor Fletcher will represent the case *for* situation ethics. Dr. Montgomery will present the case *against* situation ethics. Professor Fletcher is the author of *Situation Ethics; The New Morality*, and seven other volumes. He received a Bachelor of Arts degree from West Virginia University and Bachelor of Divinity degree from Berkeley Divinity School. He has received honorary degrees from the Berkeley Divinity School, Kenyon College and Ohio Wesleyan University. Professor Fletcher taught Social Ethics for many years at the Episcopal Theological Seminary at Cambridge, Massachusetts. He is now teaching Ethics at the University of Virginia Medical School.

11

He has preached and lectured at more than 300 colleges and universities in the world.

Our other speaker, Dr. Montgomery, has received the Degree of Doctor of Philosophy from the University of Chicago; the Doctorate of the University in Protestant Theology from the University of Strasbourg, France; Dr. Montgomery is Chairman of the Division of Church History and History of Christian thought at Trinity Evangelical Divinity School and Director of the seminary's European program at the University of Strasbourg. Among the books he has published are *The Suicide of Christian Theology* and *In Defense of Martin Luther*.

The format of the debate is as follows: Each speaker will take from twenty to forty minutes to state his position. Professor Fletcher will speak first, thirty minutes. Fifteen minutes for each speaker has been allotted for rebuttal. Again Professor Fletcher will speak first. Following the rebuttal period, the question cards in the programs which have been passed out to you, will be collected and the selection will be made from them.

While this is taking place, Professor Fletcher and Dr. Montgomery will have the opportunity to ask each other questions. Fifteen minutes has been allotted for this part of the debate. The final portion of the evening will be devoted to the questions addressed by members of the audience to Professor Fletcher and Dr. Montgomery. The debate will now begin with the presentation of Professor Fletcher's position on situation ethics. Professor Fletcher. [Applause.]

FLETCHER: Dr. McClurg, Dr. Montgomery, ladies and gentlemen. Two or three years ago, a feature writer for one of the national news services asked me to talk about situation ethics and the new morality, and in the course of answering his agenda of questions, I remember remarking only parenthetically, but at what point I no longer recall, that none of the Ten Commandments represents a normative principle for human conduct which is intrinsically valid or universally obliging regardless of the circumstances, so that, for example, in some situations theft is the right thing to do; in other situations, respect for the property of others is the right way to act. He reported this remark of mine accurately enough for his journalistic purposes and in consequence of the syndicated article's circulation, I received in ten to twelve weeks about 1,500 letters, almost all of them of protest and denunciation. Chiefly they came from the Corn, Cotton and Bible Belts, but also quite generally, and I might just remark that the more pious the writer, the more vicious the letter. [Laughter.]

Now, why all that fury and furor over a fairly explicit and reasonably uncontentious declaration of the relativity of human life, including its moral principles? I could find a paradigm (or *parable,* if you prefer) for the position I want to develop tonight in a story I picked up while lecturing in Louisville, Kentucky.

According to the local oral tradition, at the turn of the 19th century, a local Baptist association at Long Run in Jefferson County invited people from far and wide to a log rolling, and as part of the entertainment they provided their guests somebody posed a hypothetical problem of conscience. You are a settler in a frontier community and get wind of an impending Indian raid. You hide your four children. When the savages arrive, they succeed in invading the stockade and in the course of rooting around, they find three of your four children and destroy them. When they set about making an armistice and withdrawal, they ask you, the settler, if you have any more children hidden anywhere.

Problem: Do you tell the truth or do you tell a lie? And they say that the debate over this question split that community right down the middle, and the original congregation at Long Run is still known locally as the non-lying Baptists whereas the dissidents who removed themselves about twenty miles away to Flat Rock and started another association or congregation are even today known as the lying Baptists. I mean by telling this story to establish, quite candidly at the very outset, that I identify wholeheartedly with the *lying* Baptists.

I think there are no normative moral principles whatsoever which are intrinsically valid or universally obliging. I would contend that we may not absolutize the norms of human conduct or, if you like theological rhetoric, we may not make idols of any finite and relative rules of life. Whether we ought to follow a moral principle or not would, I contend, always depend upon the situation. This is, of course, a reasonably straightforward statement of ethical relativity. If we are, as I would want to reason, obliged in conscience sometimes to tell white lies, as we often call them, then in conscience we might be obliged sometimes to engage in white thefts and white fornications and white killings and white breakings of promises and the like.

If you will bear with me briefly for a

few minutes of prolegomena, there are in all ethical analysis four kinds of principles which we need to distinguish as a matter of intellectual care. First there are so-called "formal" principles. For example, the formal principle that we should always seek the good. Principles of this kind are represented in the formulas of Immanuel Kant, for example. Kant himself said that they are "empty" of content. To assert as the axiom of ethical investigation that we ought always to seek to do the good does not say, in the first place, *what* the good to be sought is, nor in the second place, *how* to seek it. But as soon as the formal principle is uttered it follows on the level of logic that we should then ask what *is* this good which is to be done. This is asking for the "substantive" principle—what is the good—and in the philosophical tradition there have been a number of optional replies. Hedonists, for example, would want to establish that the first-order value or the highest good is pleasure. For them if necessary all other relative value considerations would be subordinated to pleasure. Alternatively, some have held out for survival as first. Still others have argued that the first-order value or the substantive principle of ethical acts is social concern or, as I would prefer Christianly to phrase it, loving concern for others.

To this substantive question my own reply is that love is the *summum bonum*, the highest good and first-order value, the primary consideration to which in every act so far as we have the opportunity and the ability to make a rational analysis, we should be prepared "in the crunch" to sidetrack or subordinate other value considerations of right and wrong and good and evil, desirable and undesirable. But then having established one's own conclusion in respect to the substantive principle the reasonable man inquiring into good and evil questions asks, How am I to *do* my good? That is to say, what are the consequent, contingent and derivative norms? How is one ordinarily, usually, typically, and with some kind of statistical preponderance, to act lovingly or pleasurably, or self-seekingly, and so forth, in this, that or the other kind of ethical situation? At this level of analysis thoughtful men, reflecting on a wide range of human experience and consulting their forebears' experience as well as their own, will try to formulate some norms.

Normative principles are such as state that normally, usually and typically we ought, for example, to tell the truth. But now a fourth order of principles comes into view—"prescriptive" principles. There are those who would say that norms, at least in the case of some norms, if not all, should always and without exception be followed. To stick with our example, take truth telling. In a very sturdy fashion Immanuel Kant exemplified this kind of simplistic consistency by saying that if a mad and ruthless killer were to pursue a friend of his whom he had hidden in his house and demanded of him to know whether his proposed victim was hiding there, he would be compelled in conscience to tell him he was, and this was because it is always wrong, *intrinsically,* to tell a lie.

Now what I want to say (I hope not oversimply for the purposes of our dialogue tonight) is that the really vital debate going on ethically in the contemporary scene is not really substantive. That is the sixty-four-dollar question and it is ultimately definitive, but the serious disagreements we have just now in the field of ethics are *methodological,* around the question, How does one properly do ethics? Are our norms prescriptive? How should the moral agent determine the conscientious course of action as an ethically concerned decision maker, when he faces problematic questions?

I want to suggest that methodologically there are basically only three alternative strategies or method-options. One of them is to be seen in a story I like to remember about a friend of mine who arrived at the height of a political campaign's excitement in St. Louis and took a cab from Union Station to a hotel. They were held up at an intersection by a red light and the cab driver turned to his fare and said, "Well, sir, I don't know how it is with you but in my family, my great-grandfather and my grandfather and father before me all voted a straight Republican ticket." Thereupon my friend, who was a Republican, said, "Ah, that's fine, driver. I take it then that you're going to vote for Senator so-and-so." To which, God bless him, the driver replied, "No, sir, I ain't. There are times in every man's life when he's got to put his principles aside and do the right thing."

The three options open to conscience at work are to be simply labelled as legalism, antinomianism, and situationism. The legalist is one who enters into his moral decision-making situations armed with a more or less elaborate apparatus of guidelines and moral principles, i.e., norms. This doesn't distinguish him. What is specifically identifying about legalistic conscience is that it gives absolute and universal validity and obligation to some of its norms; for example, some well-intentioned but uncritically pious people do this with the Ten Commandments.

One of Sir Walter Scot's novels, *The Heart of Midlothian,* is about a couple of little orphan girls without any parental supervision and very apt to get into trouble. One of them, Effie, the less bright of the two, gets pregnant out of wedlock. Then she's accused of having destroyed her baby, charged with infanticide and put on trial. Very quickly an overwhelming body of circumstantial evidence pointing to her guilt builds up, so that when her older sister, Jeannie, is put on the stand, Jeannie perceives that if she were to answer the questions likely to be put to her by counsel, candidly and straightforwardly, the consequence would be simply to nail down the case against Effie more firmly *even though Jeannie knows for a fact that Effie is innocent.* Shall she tell the truth or shall she tell a lie, that is, in this situation technically commit perjury?

Scot was an incorrigible, irreversible, Calvinistic legalist of the first order. He has Jeannie tell the truth, so that Effie is convicted. And then in a sort of masturbatory strategem, he sends little Jeannie, like in the East Lynn story, traipsing through the snow, flecks of blood from her bare feet marking her path down to London-town where she manages to get a last minute reprieve. Ha! So everything is okay, see? What an absurd falsification of the infinite variety and complexity and tragedy of authentic human existence. Plain crap!

A few years ago I gave some lectures at St. Andrew's University, and I was fascinated by Scot's extraordinary gift for story telling. One of the tales that I keep remembering was about a Highlander who went down to the low country on a business trip and returned home to his cot on a Sunday afternoon. He found his little boy playing gaily in the sunlight in the field and therefore violating the Sabbath. He grabbed him by the arm to punish him, but his wife begged him not to do it. She said she had given the child permission, that he was only a lad full of life, it was a beautiful day, "and after all, didn't our Lord himself," she said to her husband, "say that the Sabbath was made for man and not man for the Sabbath?" His reply was "Yes, lass, he did, but it was in one of His weaker moments." [Laughter.]

You see, I want to argue that what that saying of Jesus about the Sabbath means is, much more profoundly, that morality was made for man and not man for morality. By any kind of hermeneutics, that is the intention of the synoptic writers.

The second option or alternative methodologically, in conscientious decision-making, is legalism's logical or polar opposite, antinomianism. If the legalist is somebody who is bound and captured and corseted by his moral principles, the impromptuist is unprincipled. Maybe the most sophisticated exponents of this kind of unprincipled decision-making in the contemporary scene are the secular existentialists. Take, for example, the last two chapters of Sartre's *Being and Nothingness* or Simone de Beauvoir's *Essay on Ambiguity* or, to come over to our American scene, that very long monograph of Hazel Barnes, *An Existentialist Ethics.* (The Barnes I mean is in the philosophy department of the University of Colorado.) These people are saying something we need to respect intellectually. They hold ontologically that by its very nature, reality or being itself is radically discontinuous. Every moment of existence as they see it is separate from what proceeded and what followed. Given this basic ontological theory of radical discontinuity, there is no logical foundation on which to generalize, to say nothing of absolutizing generalizations. They have no web of life, no connective tissue on which to generalize right and wrong or good and evil or desirable and undesirable, and therefore (let it be said to their credit) they *don't*.

In the course I used to give at the Harvard Business School on the ethics of business management, I remember somebody bringing in a case from the archives one day which included a verbatim report of a conversation between two men side by side on a lathe line. One man said to the other, "If Bill asks you to borrow a hundred dollars because he's had unexpected medical expenses lately, would you lend it to him?" His answer was, "Gosh, I don't know; how can I unless he asks me?" There's a simple untutored barnyard existentialist! In the same conversation the first man again said to the second, "How are you going to vote under the labor board's election three weeks hence, for the management or for the union?" And again the reply was, "Gosh, I don't know. I don't suppose I will until they hand me my ballot."

In between these two extremes lies situationism, the third strategy of conscience, and a mediating position in the spectrum. The situationist enters into troubling moral situations armed, like the legalist, with some wise sayings or *sophia*—some reflective generalizations about what is ordinar-

23

ily and typically the right thing to do. But unlike the legalist he refuses to absolutize in an idolatrous way any normative principle. From the other side like the antinomian or spontaneist or impromptuist, he is prepared to depart from a usually applicable generalization if in the particular case the consequence of following the rule is to minimize rather than to optimize whatever the first-order value is to which he's committed. I would want to argue that Christianly that first-order value ought to be *agape*—or neighbor love.

To conclude, the logic of this kind of ethical method results in such guideline propositions as that we ought to love people and use things and that the essence of immorality is to love things and use people. And by "things" we mean not only material objects of desire but abstractions like moral principles too. Situationism results in such characteristic propositions as that we ought to live by the law of love and never by any love of law. It holds that love ethics is infinitely superior to law ethics, so that chastity and not virginity, for example, is the Christian norm, and unmarried love is infinitely superior to married unlove, etc. In the course of our discussion tonight, the import of this rather abstract and highly streamlined statement of the case for situation theory may be brought out concretely enough to nail it down. Thank you very much. [Applause.]

McCLURG: We will now hear from Dr. Montgomery on his reactions to situation ethics. Dr. Montgomery. [Applause.]

MONTGOMERY: Dr. McClurg, Professor Fletcher, ladies and gentlemen, I wonder if you realize how historic this occasion is. It's a rare thing when a person who is associated with Boston through his career argues for a· less stringent ethical position than a person who spends most of his time in France.

Our task is the critical examination of Joseph Fletcher's theological ethic, a position which its creator has baptized "situation ethics" or "the new morality." This viewpoint is perhaps best summarized in terms of the six "propositions" (not "principles," "rules," or "laws," to be sure!) by which Professor Fletcher first presented his thesis to the general public (*Situation Ethics*, 1966), and which he reiterated as the point of departure for his later work on the practical application of the new morality (*Moral Responsibility*, 1967):

   I. Only one thing is intrinsically good, namely, love: nothing else.
  II. The ultimate norm of Christian decisions is love: nothing else.
 III. Love and justice are the same, for justice is love distributed.

IV. Love wills the neighbor's good whether we like him or not.
V. Only the end justifies the means: nothing else.
VI. Decisions ought to be made situationally, not prescriptively.

Leaving aside fascinating textual questions, such as the presence of quotation marks around "thing" in proposition I. as originally set out in 1966, and their disappearance in the 1967 restatement (a manifestation of what philosopher W. H. Dray calls "hardening of the categories"? a Freudian slip suggesting that Fletcher himself is not clear on what love in fact *is*?), we should accompany these propositions with a succinct statement of their implications (Fletcher, "Why 'New'?" *Religion in Life,* Spring, 1966):

In some situations unmarried love could be infinitely more moral than married unlove, as when the parties to a marriage exercise their legal rights of sexual access without the tenderness and concern which alone validate sexual lovemaking. Lying could be more Christian than telling the truth, since the only "virtue" in telling the truth is telling it in love. Stealing could be better than respecting private property if, as in eminent domain, the private ownership denies the greatest love of the greatest number. No action is good or right of itself. It depends on whether it hurts or helps people, whether it serves love's purpose (understanding love to be concern for persons) *in the situation.*

The new morality, in short, subordinates principles to circumstances, the general to the particular, and forces the "natural" and the "scriptural" to give way to the personal and the actual.

Two obvious critical questions demand attention as soon as this ethic of "act agapeism" is stated: Is it New? and Is it Morality? Tempted as we might be to pursue the historical question as to how innovative Professor Fletcher's view is, we must forego it, noting only the sound observation by John M. Gessell that "American morality has always been 'new' morality, and pragmatism has usually been substituted for principles in the American ethical experience" (*Anglican Theological Review,* January, 1968; cf. Edward Long, "The History and Literature of 'The New Morality,'" in *The Situation Ethics Debate,* ed. Harvey Cox [1968]). To focus on the true origins of situation ethics might lead us into the genetic fallacy, wherein origins are allowed to determine worth—a fallacy Professor Fletcher himself seems to court in his constant stress on the alleged "newness" of his position. After all, one must not forget that the valuable discovery of ammonia occurred when the alchemist Brandt boiled toads in urine; our concern is to see what bubbles to the surface when ethical alchemist Fletcher boils love in the cauldron of situations. Is genuine morality the product of the distillation? Or have the fumes of the situational brew so fogged the experimenter's mental and spiritual sensitivities that he is unable to distinguish responsibility from irresponsibility, ethical maturity from immaturity? To engage in such an analysis is simultaneously an easy and a very difficult task.

Criticism Easy and Difficult

The evaluation of Fletcherian situationalism might seem, at first glance, a facile operation. The ideology received its direct statement but five years ago, has (like its dystheological counterparts, the Pike-Robinson-Vidler "radical theology," and the death-of-God movement) had virtually no serious impact outside England and America, and even in the English-speaking world has been ignored by professional philosophers (witness the absence of reviews or critical appraisals of the subject in the journals devoted to philosophical ethics). Discussion of situation morality has been limited to American and British theological circles, largely to those of liberal and neo-orthodox orientation at that; and the critic's problems are lessened even more by the collection of a large number of the ephemeral theological reviews in parasitic—or symbiotic?—compendia that live off the original book (*The Situation Ethics Debate; Storm over Ethics* [1967]). The powerfully negative tone of much of the reaction to Professor Fletcher's views offers a critic a veritable *embarras de richesses.* One wonders, for example, how detailed a critique of a book is warranted when James M. Gustafson can write (*Christian Century,* May 18, 1966—in a passage strangely omitted by Cox in the reprint of Gustafson's review in *The Situation Ethics Debate*!):

> It [*Situation Ethics*] is made up too much of assertions, observations, preachments, stale jokes, significant cases that could have been the subject of more extensive arguments, sometimes dubious historical allusions (e.g., can one quote Augustine's "Love God, and do what you please" while at the same time attacking the theory of the virtues that makes the statement significant in Augustine's framework?) and loose use of words.

Or what can be added to the perceptive observation of Robert V. Smith of Colgate (*Journal of the American Academy of Religion,* March, 1967)?

Ethical theory is no more advanced by the

slogans of *Situation Ethics* than is theological reflection by the slogans of *Honest to God*. . . . Fletcher does not succeed in showing how this [agape-love] principle contributes to an effective method of ethical decision-making. His confessed desire to outrun the dangers of legalism permits him to fall headlong into the arms of emptiness. This emptiness is present even though he gives numerous cases and tells many anecdotes. He makes his opposition to any form of rules, principles, maxims or laws overwhelmingly clear, but in spite of constant references to love he leaves one unsure of what love is and of what it might mean to "do love," as he puts it.

At the same time, criticism of the Fletcherian viewpoint—especially in dialogal context—is almost impossibly difficult, not merely in practice but also in principle. Here I do not refer primarily to what Gustafson has accurately termed Professor Fletcher's bent toward "verbal pyrotechnics"—the quality that a theological reporter of his dialogue with molecular biologist French Anderson at the National Cathedral, Washington, D.C., described as having manifested itself in "nearly two hours of biting sarcasm" (*Christianity Today*, April 10, 1970). This roadblock could certainly be overcome by men of good will (or by a 250 lb. moderator). Far more significant is the built-in problem of debating anyone who holds that "only the end justifies the means: nothing else" (proposition V., it will be recalled). Here we find ourselves squarely in the philosophical quagmire inherent in situationalism—a quagmire in which the critic of the new morality finds himself inevitably stuck as soon as he offers battle.

Ends, Means and Truth-Telling

The insurmountable difficulty is simply this: there is no way, short of sodium pentothal, of knowing when the situationist is actually endeavoring to set forth genuine facts and true opinions, and when he is lying like a trooper. Why? because deception is allowed on principle by the new morality, as long as the ultimate aim is love. Consider: if Professor Fletcher acts consistently with his premises, and if he should consider it an act of true love toward me or toward the audience (i.e., if he should consider it to our good as his neighbors— principle IV.) to convince us of the superiority of situation ethics, he can to this end introduce any degree of factual misinformation, rhetorical pettifogging, or direct prevarication into the discussion. On the other hand, if he should solemnly promise us that under all circumstances in the present dialogue he will tell the truth, the whole truth, and nothing but the truth, he would suddenly become a deontological contradictor of his own propositions (for the neighbor's good in love would no longer justify deviations from truth).

But wait! Should he assure us, by swearing on his mother's grave, etc., that he *will* tell us the truth no matter what, can we even then relax our vigilance? After all, *that very assurance* may well be a situationally justified prevarication for the sake of "doing us good in love" by convincing us of the merits of situationalism. This brings us necessarily to a corollary of the ancient logical conundrum, treated at length by Bertrand Russell and others: "If a Cretan tells you that all Cretans are liars, can you believe him?" Our restatement goes: "If a situation ethicist, holding to the proposition that the end justifies the means in love, tells you that he is not lying, can you believe him?"

This agonizing problem, it must be emphasized, is not of the theoretical, academic variety; it cuts to the very heart of practical existence. Beginning with the immediate, it leaves me the protagonist and you the audience entirely incapable of ever being sure that Professor Fletcher means what he says. Now consider what would be involved if such situationalism became normative in principle in our society (I say "in principle," for there are already sobering indicators of its widespread employment in practice). The very legal structures essential for the maintenance of organized community life would become inoperable, for no man's testimony would necessarily be worth listening to.

This is why even Rousseau suddenly became intensely religious in the *Contrat social* when he stated (IV.8) that citizenship in his ideal state would be granted only to those who believed in God and a judgment after death: having the fortune to live prior to the onset of the new morality, Rousseau felt that belief in God would insure absolute moral standards and meaningful oath-taking in the courts. And since mutual trust is the basis not only of institutions of justice but also of economic life (money itself is little more than a symbol of mutual confidence, as every inflation and depression illustrates), community relationships, and all other societal phenomena, the adoption of the Fletcherian ethic would let loose on society in general the same dragon of chaos that is conjured up on a limited scale in a debate like this with one whose principles do not compel him to truth-telling. Paul Ramsey of Princeton has driven this point home by illustrations from the sphere of personal obligation ("The Biblical Norm of Right-eousness," *Interpretation,* October, 1970):

> If a person genuinely means to attach an exception-making criterion to his promises or to his marriage vow, if he means to live by a rule of practice which states that the marriage covenant holds, that promises should be kept except when by a direct appeal to what Christian love requires it would be better *not* to keep them, he had better say so, since the one he promises or his marriage partner (unless they are Fletcherites who have been briefed) will not understand it that way! If you promise a dying friend, no one else knowing, to take care of his children, *why should you do so* if two other children come along who are more intelligent and whose care and nurture by you would do more good? If a person means to get married for better, in health and in prosperity, and has some reservation about the worse, in sickness, poverty, and adversity he had better say so, since one's partner will not understand it that way—unless he or she is a latter-day consequentialist whose marriage was in the first place a *bargain* founded upon a calculus of doing the most good on the whole. Thus, there are such things as fairness and justice, promises made, and marriage covenants established, concerning which one should do more than ask, which unique situational decision or particular action would exhibit the most love?

Not a single aspect of human society—

from regular garbage collection and public
library book-borrowing through friendship
and marriage to equal protection under the
law and the search for truth in institutions
of higher learning such as this one—could
survive the general onset of situation ethics.
The immaturity of the new morality dis-
plays itself first of all in its lack of recog-
nition of the truth so well expressed by
Ferdinand Lassalle and quoted by Arthur
Koestler: "Ends and means on earth are
so entangled / that changing one you change
the other too." Thus analytical philosopher
Antony Flew shrewdly observes, in his essay on "Ends and Means" (*The Encyclo-
pedia of Philosophy,* ed. Paul Edwards
[1967]), that "the reluctant inquisitor,
Ivanov, of Koestler's *Darkness at Noon*
may be transformed by the processes of
habituation into the exultant O'Brien of
George Orwell's appalling nightmare,
1984."

Love as Panacea

But, it will immediately be objected,
such negative possibilities are surely ex-
cluded by the fact that in Fletcherian
morality love constitutes the "only intrinsic good" and "ultimate norm." In *1984*,
as O'Brien expressly declares, the end to
be sought by any effective means is power;

love could hardly produce a comparable cacatopia.

Here the critic of the new morality must exercise utmost care, particularly in circles where "make love, not war" stickers have proliferated. Not to hold love as the solution to anything and everything is often the equivalent in the 1970s of the denigration of motherhood and the flag in the 1870s. Let me suggest, however, that "love," the keystone of Professor Fletcher's situationalism, functions as a prime example of what Richard Weaver, in his work, *The Ethics of Rhetoric* (1953), calls "charismatic terms": "These terms seem to have broken loose somehow and to operate independently of referential connections. . . . Their meaning seems inexplicable unless we accept the hypothesis that their content proceeds out of a popular will that they *shall* mean something."

At first glance, Professor Fletcher seems to give love a degree of specific content. He makes much of the example of Jesus and seems at times to define love, much as Charles M. Sheldon did in his romantic-moralistic novels, *In His Steps* and *What Would Jesus Do?*, as the equivalent of Jesus' teaching and practice. But it is manifestly clear that Professor Fletcher's understanding of love and morality does not derive from the Bible in general or from Jesus' ministry in particular. Professor Fletcher never tires of condemning alleged "biblical legalism," and in spite of the extensive work done by Gustaf Wingren and others in refuting the anti-law extremism of Barthian and Lundensian theology (e.g., the negative attitude toward the nomos motif in Nygren's *Agape and Eros*), Fletcher remains virtually a mid-20th century Marcionite. Moreover, his acceptance of radical techniques of New Testament criticism removes any real possibility of his identifying the ethic of Jesus; were he to take the entire New Testament picture seriously, he would find—as any number of his critics have shown—that the New Testament, no less than the Old, insists on absolute moral standards.

British theologian Ernest F. Kevan (author of the significantly titled work, *The Grace of Law*) well summarized this point in his Tyndale Biblical Theology Lecture of July 4, 1955: "There is no hint anywhere in the New Testament that the Law has lost its validity in the slightest degree, nor is there any suggestion of its repeal. On the contrary, the New Testament teaches unambiguously that the Ten Commandments are still binding upon all men." To re-introduce an earlier concrete example, it is difficult to believe that the Jesus who called himself "the Truth," condemned his opponents for lying, and connected prevarication with the work of the devil himself ("you are of your father the devil, and your will is to do your father's desires; ... when he lies, he speaks according to his own nature, for he is a liar and the father of lies"—John 8:44), is the source of the Fletcherian assertion: "Lying could be more Christian than telling the truth, since the only 'virtue' in telling the truth is telling it in love."

Alternatively, Professor Fletcher seems to give love content by equating love and justice ("love and justice are the same"— proposition III.), but we quickly see that instead of allowing justice to inform love (as Socrates strove to do in Plato's *Republic*), justice is absorbed into the ambiguities of love ("justice is love distributed"). This identification of justice with love is in fact a colossal example of what contemporary philosophy terms the "category mistake"— the confusion of categories. Gilbert Ryle's example, in *The Concept of Mind,* of the confusion of a legal entity (Oxford University) with its concrete component colleges (American visitor: "I've seen all your colleges, yes, but *where is the university?*) can be directly paralleled with Fletcher's belief that justice and love are identical. Even the hymn writer Bonar (and hymn writers are not particularly known for philosophical astuteness) understood this distinction, long before the onset of situationism:

> Will they tell us what is to regulate service, if not law? *Love,* they say. This is a pure fallacy. Love is not a *rule,* but a *motive.* Love does not tell me *what* to do, it tells me *how* to do it. . . . Love without law to guide its impulses would be the parent of will-worship and confusion, as surely as terror and self-righteousness, unless upon the supposition of an inward miraculous illumination, as an equivalent for law.

Finally, Professor Fletcher offers what seems to be the most specific description of love his situationism is capable of providing: "Love wills the neighbor's good whether we like him or not" (proposition IV.). Here we suddenly discover that the Fletcherian "act-agapeism" reduces to a utilitarian ethic of the Bentham-Mill variety, with a heavy dose of theological charisma added to improve the flavor. But the *bête noire* that has plagued utilitarianism now leaps upon situationalism to devour it, and the theological flavoring only makes the dish more appetizing. For neither utilitarianism nor the new morality is capable of satisfactorily answering the essential questions: "*which* neighbor's good?" and "just what *constitutes* my neighbor's good?" Since these questions have to be answered, either explicitly or implicitly, in every ethical action, one finds the situationist continually importing answers to them into his moral decisions by way of unrecognized and unjustified value judgments. The alleged demon of explicit code ethics is exorcised by the new morality, only to return with seven of his friends—the devils of implicit, "self-evident" principles—and the last state of morality is considerably worse than the first. Let us note some specific examples.

In a trenchant essay on "Moral Consistency" in the *Journal of Religious Thought* (Vol. XXIII, No. 2 [1966-67]), Carol Murphy writes:

> At one place, Dr. Fletcher refers to the situation of Judith lying to Holofernes and using her sex-allure to murder him "to save Israel." The apocryphal writer praises her; this is said to be "a sturdy ethical evaluation of Judith's situational action." Many questions arise: Is not Holofernes a neighbor to be loved? Is he merely to be used for an ethnic abstraction? How can love draw a circle that leaves him out? ... Sincere sacrifices have been made to idols, and no doubt

those who threw children to Moloch had the best intentions.

So, perhaps, did Caiaphas when he judged it expedient that "one man should die for the people, and that the whole nation perish not." The calculus of the greatest good for the greatest number, which Dr. Fletcher calls the "agapaic calculus," is one of the strongest temptations to the moralist. In its name assassinations have been committed (Dr. Fletcher would have approved of Hitler's assassination; but what about those of Franz Ferdinand and Gandhi, also "justified" by a zealous calculus?), and the interests of a few have been exploited, as the Scottsboro boys were by the Communist Party, for "larger" ends. It is hard to see how any decision can be made free from demonic elements that does not hold to the deeper organic unity of both the few and the many. As far as calculus goes, incidentally, it is possible to conclude that if one life is infinitely precious, one infinity is equal to a million infinities.

The same implicit introduction of value judgments as to the *true* neighbor and what is *truly* good for him can be seen in Fletcher's treatment of the ethics of abortion. Paul Ramsey observes that "even in *Situation Ethics* one comes upon at least one general rule of behavior, or general principle of ethics, besides love itself: . . . 'No unwanted or unintended baby should ever be born'" (*Deeds and Rules in Christian Ethics* [1967]. p. 168). Clearly there is nothing inherent in the idea of love that excludes babies from the sphere of "neighbor" (one ought rather to argue the contrary from Jesus' declaration that "of such is the kingdom of heaven"!); and it is fairly evident that Professor Fletcher has not checked with the babies in question to obtain their views on the subject. The principle that the unborn child is of less "neighbor value" than adult society is a gratuitous importation of value (dysvalue?) into a situation where love most certainly does not have all the answers. Love, as Bonar reminded us, requires principles to "guide its impulses"; either the principles will be explicit and justifiable, or they will be hidden and perhaps terrifying: like Caiaphas' exclusion of Christ from the sphere of neighbor love, or the abortionist's rejection of the unborn child.

A Radical Proposal: Morals not Mores

Ours is a time of staggering ethical crisis. Issues such as abortion and the rights of racial and minority groups are being faced by all segments of the population for perhaps the first time in our entire national history. A new consciousness of the need for soundly-based ethical principles has arisen. Ironically, however, at this very time of need, Christian theology appears to be offering little more than what Professor Tom Driver has called the "free-floating ideal" of new morality ("Love Needs Law," *Religion in Life*, Spring, 1966). The result has been the adoption of arbitrary absolutes by a revolutionary generation which recognizes its imperative need for permanent ideals, but which sees no way to justify them. Sidney Hook has observed that " 'natural law' may be out but 'absolute human rights' are in" (Kiefer and Munitz [eds.], *Ethics and Social Justice* [1970], p. 76). Unfortunately, arbitrary absolutes are a most dangerous commodity, for the love of one moment can become the hate of the next; and blind zeal for racial justice in the America of the 1970s may not differ motivationally from blind zeal for racism in the Germany of the 1930s.

What is required above all is a proper justification of "absolute human rights," but where can this be found? If one follows the course of 20th century philosophical ethics, one is led to a very sobering conclusion—the conclusion reached by Wittgenstein at the end of his *Tractatus Logico-Philosophicus*: "Ethics is transcendental" (6.421). That is to say, all human attempts to create value are necessarily conditioned by the human predicament and reflect the limitations and prejudices from which they arise. The only ethic that could, even in principle, stand above such societal limits and establish "absolute human rights" would be an ethic that derived, not from finite situations, but from the realm of the transcendent.

This is precisely the claim of the historic Christian faith: that biblical revelation constitutes a transcendent word from God establishing ethical values once for all. The superiority of such a revelatory ethic over contemporary situationalism can be seen in at least four areas: (1) Love is expressly defined in terms of God's nature, as revealed in Scripture, and is justified in terms of His very being. Thus love is not allowed to dissipate like a Homeric wraith through its confusion with utilitarian vageries. (2) Absolute moral principles are explicitly set forth; these inform love and guide its exercise. Standards of truth and justice— such as the absolute equality of the races (Galatians 3:28)—are placed above the shifting sands of situational change and are guaranteed against societal and ideological pressures. (3) A final judgment on evil is assured. Thus no man ultimately "gets away" with evil, and moral struggle in history becomes something far different from "a tale told by an idiot, full of sound and fury, signifying nothing." Situations are not only judged by absolute principle in this life; they will be so judged in the next. (4) A remedy is provided for the root problem in the human ethical dilemma: man's selfishness. Biblical revelation offers to all those who are willing to face their self-centeredness and seek Christ's healing the gift of "new creaturehood" (II Corinthians 5:17) and the living presence of God the Holy Spirit in them to conform them to the image of Christ's holiness (II Corinthians 3:18). Only a revolutionary change in man can produce a revolution in social morality; it is the great strength of biblical ethics that it offers just such a change for the asking.

Perhaps the saddest aspect of the new morality is thrown into sharp relief at this point: though purportedly a *theological* ethic, situationalism has little appreciation of the central theological verities. "Some critics," writes Professor Fletcher in his own defense (*The Situation Ethics Debate*, ed. Cox, p. 256), "have been shrewd enough to recognize that situationism is, by traditional standards, a little 'weak' on the side of guilt, 'sin,' repentance, and forgiveness." To Christian psychologist Wayne Oates,

Fletcher said: "I really do not think you have said anything when you say that the Holy Spirit is at work in human decision. On this I am an agnostic." Commented Oates: "He says he is agnostic as to the Holy Spirit. He says that love *is* the Holy Spirit. In fact, one wonders if his doctrine of God is not either Unitarian or binitarian" ("The New Morality: A Psychological and Theological Critique," *Review and Expositor,* Summer, 1967). It is just such theological weakness that keeps Professor Fletcher from seeing the true significance of the ambiguous ethical situations he continually cites in opposing the absolute ethic of biblical revelation. In the published dialogue with Roman Catholics Thomas Wassmer and William May (*Hello, Young Lovers* [1970]), he presses May to admit that he might torture a prisoner to obtain information that would save innocent lives. Dr. May: "I might do the act even though I thought that it were evil. I believe that human beings sometimes knowingly do things that they know to be wrong, acts for which they will be sorry and, if Catholics, matters for confession."

Here the ways divide between situationalism and the historic ethic of the Christian church, Protestant and Catholic. Dr. May, over against Professor Fletcher, saw clearly that when sinful human situations require a choice to be made between conflicting absolute moral demands, the trouble lies not with the demands but with the situations. In these cases, the "lesser" of evils may have to be accepted, but it is still in every sense an evil and must drive the Christian to the Cross for forgiveness and to the Holy Spirit for restoration. The law, as the Apostle insists, acts as "a servant [*paidagogos*: the Greek or Roman slave who tutored the child] to bring us to Christ" (Galatians 3:24); where the divine law is dethroned, men invariably come to believe that they can justify themselves in their moral decisions, and they lose their way to the Cross.

This, we believe, is the Fletcherian tragedy: ethics has become a device for self-justification through the very sinful human situations that ought to lead selfish humans to the one source of true forgiveness and life. We plead with Professor Fletcher, in an age crying out for unambiguous ethical principles as the only foundation of human dignity, to cease the irresponsible practice of sticking his thumb into sinful human situations, pulling out the plum of moral self-vindication, and saying, "what a good boy am I." This theological, philosophical, and social immaturity cannot be tolerated;

the issues are too grave and the time to solve them too limited. Rather, may we all allow the absolute moral demands of a holy God—those expressions of his very will which stand above the flux of situational change—to drive us to the Cross, where (thank heaven!) ethical renewal is still possible.

McCLURG: We have now come to the period of rebuttal. Each speaker has been allotted 15 minutes, and Professor Fletcher will speak first. Professor Fletcher.

FLETCHER: Thank you, Dr. McClurg. I think we haven't just now reached the stage of rebuttal—we've heard 35-40 minutes of it! In the course of Dr. Montgomery's very carefully and somewhat emotionally prepared material, he's brought out any number of exciting hares worth pursuing. But our time is limited and I'm eager to get out 'there' in the audience and hear the feedback. Selfishly regarded, that is when I get my profits in these sessions. So rather than try seriatim to run over a number of points made by Dr. Montgomery, which I did note here on a piece of paper, I think that I won't try to refute a number of his question-begging statements and his use of epithets sometimes as substitutes for analysis. Let's try to find out in a very down-to-earth and basic fashion not only why he doesn't just disagree but why he feels so strongly that he couldn't get around to explaining why. Therefore, rather than using the time offered, Dr. McClurg, let's hear more from Dr. Montgomery in answer to a kind of package question. Are you saying, sir, that we must in conscience always tell the truth? And if there are any exceptions, when might we prevaricate and why? And along with that, are you saying that tyrannicide is never justifiable? If it might be, when and why? And in the same vein, were you or weren't you saying that interruptions of pregnancy are always wrong? But if there are times when it might be done, why would it be? You see, you wrapped up your commentary by saying that what is really quite vitally needed in our times is (I think this is a correct record of it) a proper justification of absolute human rights, and I suppose the desire to justify absolute rights would go along with the desire to justify absolute norms. But, unless I've misread my material, Christian ethics and moral theology and casuistry have never allowed that human rights are anything but, to use the technical language of the trade, "imperfect," that is to say, they are relative and contingent. Is it always wrong to have

an abortion? Is it always wrong to kill
tyrants? Is it always wrong to tell lies?
Not just quick replies but elaborate a little
bit. Tell us how you would answer these
questions and the reasons.

MONTGOMERY: The first part of this
package question is, "Why do I feel so
strongly about this problem?" I think that
I made that very clear in my presentation;
and I think, Professor Fletcher, that you
caught it quite well. The need for dealing
with questions of human rights at the present time is of such a magnitude that when
I see anyone in a position of influence claim
that there are not intrinsically evil acts,
I become extremely worried. I've given
numerous illustrations in my paper of what
would occur if the kind of approach you're
suggesting were to become normative in
our society. This, in my opinion, would
create a nightmare condition; and if I'm
even half right, then I think I've got every
reason to be disturbed.

As to the specific questions, "Must one
never lie? Must one never kill a tyrant?
Must one never be an instrument in an
abortion?", the answer is, in terms of what
is right: "No." One must not tell lies; one
must not kill other people; one must not
abort." Now, if you're saying, "Will you

then under no circumstances do these things?" my answer to this is the same answer that Dr. May gave:[1] "It may be that I am forced to do this, but if so, I am still committing wrong." In my judgment, the greatest difficulty in situation ethics is revealed at exactly this point. The situation ethicist properly recognizes the ambiguity of situations and the extreme difficulty, often, in knowing what ought to be done; but he endeavors, in these situations, to *justify himself*. In terms of the ethical approach that I outlined, one *cannot* so justify oneself. If, concretely, I were put in the position that you described of either informing a killer as to where a child was hidden or lying about it, it's conceivable that I would have to lie. But if I did so, I would be unable to justify this ethically; in short, I would be unable to get off the hook. In Christian terminology, I would have committed a sin which should drive me to the Cross for forgiveness. This is what I find almost totally lacking in your writings: no one is driven to the Cross. Everybody ends up justified in these situations, and I think the reason for this is very simple. I don't think that you have

---

[1] In *Hello, Young Lovers.*

any serious doctrine of sin nor any serious understanding of Christ's redemptive work. These central theological verities just don't appear in your ethics. What you present is a utilitarianism with a kind of "Jesus flavoring" to it.

FLETCHER: Is it in order now for me to comment? Am I being heard all right? You've spoken of a kind of fatal defect or inherent contradiction or weakness in situation ethics, but I don't think you answered my question, which was a very earthy down-to-cases kind of question (where I think all of these problems, even theoretically, must be decided). In my view, you reveal the inherent defect and weakness of "law morality," for you have said in reply to my question "Is it always wrong to have an abortion?"—"Yes, it always is." It seems to me absolutely unbelievable that anybody could say that. And then you say, "But if one were the instrument of an abortion, which one might be on some occasions (you didn't say what), then one would be doing the wrong thing." Since the tragic complexities of life sometimes call us to do what we might call the "lesser evil," you *would* be an instrument because the alternative to the abortion would be greater evil than the evil of the abortion. Now, this is very helpful and it's right on target because it's asking us to think about the issues that are at stake, at a rather fundamental and even elemental level. For, you see, the issue then arises, where do we place the locus of value? Wherein is a human act right or wrong? Good or evil? Is the rightness or the wrongness of an act inherent and intrinsic in the act itself, so that it is right or wrong according to its classification? Or is an act right or wrong extrinsically according to the context of the contingent circumstances? It's always dangerous to do another man's thinking for him, but it appears to me that what Dr. Montgomery is saying is that whether anything we do is right or wrong is determined by the act itself; that some things are inherently and intrinsically evil, although in some situations when it appears to the conscientious decision-maker to be a lesser evil than the alternative, one would somehow be justified in doing it.

It is ethically foolish to say we "ought" to do what is wrong! What I want to argue philosophically, with respect to the issue over the locus of value in human acts, is that the rightness or the wrongness of anything we do is extrinsic, relative, and dependent upon the circumstances, so that to have an abortion out of loving concern for everybody's best interests involved, is not an excusably evil thing to do, but a good thing to do. And therefore, the basic issue at stake here might well be over this question of, "How are acts validated in the forum of conscience, intrinsically or extrinsically?" And what I want to contend for is the view that if I tell a lie for love's sake (and I don't think we tell the truth for truth's sake—I think we tell the truth for love's sake), then I haven't committed a sin for which I'm to beat my breasts, you know, in self-accusation, *Mea culpa, peccavi, peccavi,*[1] but rather I'm to say that having acted out of love I've done the *right* thing!

MONTGOMERY: Yes, this is exactly the question—and how are we going to determine it? Will we, as Christian theologians, go to Jesus to see how he handles such problems? Are we going to attempt to determine whether or not he sets forth absolutes which, when violated, definitely mean that the violator ought to employ the *Mea culpa*? That's the issue; and, as far as I can see, your answer to this is that because you don't see any absolute

---

[1] "The guilt is mine": a traditional expression of personal contrition in Latin theology.

principles, there aren't any. What do you do with the teaching and example of Jesus? I think your approach has already become evident. You do with Jesus what Luther said some of the scholastics did with the Bible just before the Reformation: you turn him into a wax nose that can be twisted in any direction. Where he doesn't agree with your teaching on love, he falls by the wayside. What kind of obligation do you feel to accord yourself with the approach Jesus takes on ethical matters?

FLETCHER: You speak as if there were a simple consensus and a rather obvious one about what Jesus said and taught and intended. And this is just not true. And I have to say in all candor that when I examine the Gospel account of Jesus' teaching in the light of our question, the first thing that strikes me is that he said nothing directly or even implicitly about it one way or another. Jesus was a simple Jewish peasant. He had no more philosophical sophistication than a guinea pig, and I don't turn to Jesus for philosophical sophistication.

MONTGOMERY: Well, sir, I think that's your trouble. [Laughter and applause from audience.]

McCLURG: The format of the debate seems to have deteriorated somewhat! I think this might be an appropriate occasion for questions to be collected, and while they're being collected and sorted, Professor Fletcher and Dr. Montgomery can continue this dialogue.

MONTGOMERY: I didn't intend my last comment as a kind of slam or a play to the audience. I'm very serious about this. To illustrate: your handling of the Gospel incident concerning distribution of money to the poor vs. the use of costly ointment[1] plainly shows that you're operating with a prior standard as to whether or not standards exist. This prior assumption determines your interpretation of the New Testament. You do not arrive at your view because contemporary critical analysis of the New Testament rejects Jesus' remarks on that occasion; there is no question of "textual weakness" in the passages. In point of fact, if you question those remarks of Jesus, you also have to question *in the very same documents* the material which you cite in support of your position. You practice what is known theologically as "eisegesis" instead of exegesis. In other words, instead of getting your theology out

---

[1] Matt. 26:6-13; Mark 14:3-9; John 12:1-8.

of New Testament material, you force your theology into the New Testament and where the Bible doesn't agree, it loses out.

FLETCHER: No, I can't accept that way of characterizing my understanding and interpretation—my hermeneutics.

MONTGOMERY: Well, would you explain in that concrete instance how you arrived at the conclusion that we are not in any way obligated to accept what is reported as a genuine saying of Jesus?

FLETCHER: Yes, I think that that saying of Jesus, as we find it here in presumably the best texts available to us, is so inconsistent with so much else that he has to say, that it becomes suspect—just as I think that Jesus' "divorce teaching" is suspect. Almost invariably, if I appreciate the mood and the ethos of Jesus' teaching in the accounts, he speaks not like the Torah or law-minded moralists or Pharisees of his day in terms of precepts, but rather in terms of broad ideals and principles. Then suddenly on this particular score we find him, with the one possible "Matthean exception" in the first Gospel, saying divorce is always wrong because marriages are inherently eternal.[1] He doesn't absolu-

---

[1] Matt. 5:32 and 19:9, also Luke 16:18.

tize any other moral guideline like that. And so therefore, Dr. Montgomery, I, like a great many Christian people today, believe that there are situations in which the most loving thing to do, tragic as divorces are, is to break some marriages. I just cannot see . . . Are you asking me, as a fellow Christian, to take everything that is recorded in the Gospels as being Jesus' utterance, literally and absolutely? How do you deal with this troubling problem of divorce?

MONTGOMERY: It is perfectly clear that Jesus' statements on the subject of divorce are contained in the very same historical material that gives me my general picture of him. If the material is suspect in regard to a particular item of this kind, then I would have great difficulty in building up any kind of picture of Jesus which I could use for ethics or anything else. Moreover, this teaching on divorce is by no means inconsistent with his general teaching. For example, consider one of the key passages in the Sermon on the Mount, which I alluded to before: "Whosoever therefore shall break one of these least commandments, and shall teach men so, he shall be called the least in the kingdom of heaven: but whosoever shall do and teach them, the same shall be called great in the kingdom of heaven." [1]

FLETCHER: Yes. So?

MONTGOMERY: Now, if this isn't the statement of somebody who holds to intrinsic morality, I'd like to know what he could possibly have said to convince you.

FLETCHER: Then how do you view that highly Jewish passage in the first Gospel— how do you . . . ?

MONTGOMERY: Most of the passages were Jewish. He was Jewish.

FLETCHER: Yes, of course. That's my point. And as a Jew he was a real bust out and a rebel against the legalism of his people. He was in rebellion against Torah[2] and he took the war right to the very heart of authentic Jewish piety, for example, by saying to his hearers, "Look, the whole law teaches us that the shewbread—in modern Christian language, the reserved sacrament—is to be handled only according to the rules and by the priests. But I say unto you, don't forget about Moses

---

[1] Matt. 5:19.
[2] The Old Testament Law; more specifically, the first five books of the Old Testament (Genesis through Deuteronomy).

and what he did with his fighting men.
If somebody's hungry, never hesitate. Go
in, as it were, into the holy place. Take
out the shewbread and eat it until human
need is satisfied. Forget the Law."

MONTGOMERY: Now I'm very glad that
you brought up that illustration, for it shows
something extremely important in this matter of determining what Jesus is for and
what he's against. He is *not* against the
Torah and what he opposes in the instances
you cite does not happen to be the teaching
of the Torah. It was rather a traditional,
Mishnaic legalism characteristic of Old
Testament religion during the period between the giving of the Torah and Jesus'
own teaching. This can readily be seen simply by checking Strack and Billerbeck's
commentary on the teachings of Jesus in
the light of the Mishnah.[1] If you examine
every one of the biblical passages cited
in your book *Situation Ethics* to show that
Jesus is opposing the Torah, you'll find
that all these so-called oppositions to the

[1] H. L. Strack and P. Billerbeck, *Kommentar zum
Neuen Testament aus Talmud und Midrasch* (5 vols.;
Munich: C. H. Beck, 1922-1956), in loco. The Talmud
is the great collection of extra-biblical Jewish legal
traditions; it is composed of the Mishnah (the oral
law, compilation of which was achieved by 2nd century A.D. by Rabbi Judah the Prince) and the Gema-
ra (later rabbinic commentaries on the Mishnah).

Torah are oppositions to legalistic accretions or attitudes *subsequent* to the setting forth of the Torah itself. In other words, Jesus is trying to peel away the traditions of the Jews that obscured the original teaching given to them.

FLETCHER: Yes, like the *Corban* thing.[1] Good. I'm glad that now we've said one thing at least that we're agreed on.

MONTGOMERY: Can we pursue that?

FLETCHER: I beg your pardon . . .

MONTGOMERY: I'm sorry; go ahead. I didn't want to interrupt you.

FLETCHER: We can push it back, I think, a little bit farther than that. I would want to reason that Jesus was attempting to get back behind the legalism that developed in and after the Exile to the kind of prophetic freedom and responsibility that characterized Judaism in its earlier stages, when law was thought of, not as code, but as a way of life.

MONTGOMERY: Then why does he place so much stress on not breaking the least of these commandments? And why

---

[1] Mark 7:1-13.

does he give illustration after illustration from the commandments of what people ought to do? Why does he even speak of love in terms of the fulfilling of the Law?

FLETCHER: I think a more careful way of making your point would be to ask me, why do these writers put their memory of what Jesus had to say in that very legalistic way?

MONTGOMERY: All right, I'll ask you the very same thing. In the case of the passages *you* cite from Jesus, why can't we say that the New Testament community has imposed its ideas upon Jesus? You see, this absolutely begs the question. With your approach, there isn't a single thing in Jesus' teaching which couldn't be dismissed as "an imposition upon his original teaching by the community"—and the peculiar thing is that in your writings the things that are always imposed by the community on Jesus are the things *you disagree with*!

FLETCHER: How does it happen that we were assigned to discuss the problem of situation ethics and we find ourselves arguing about exegetics and hermeneutics? [1] Why all this biblicist business?

---

[1] I.e., questions of biblical interpretation.

MONTGOMERY Perhaps because this has something to do with Christian theology? [Laughter and applause from audience.]

FLETCHER: Then let me ask why an obvious remark like that brings forth such gushes of strange joy?

MONTGOMERY: Dear me, I don't know. [Continued laughter from audience.]

McCLURG: It looks like we're beginning to have audience participation. [Laughter.]

McCLURG: We have scheduled time for questions from the audience, but we don't have time for a great many. It might be well to begin with a question to Professor Fletcher. The question is very short: "Who is Jesus?"

FLETCHER: That sounds like an Evangelical trying to get a confession of faith. [Laughter.] Oh well, I know this is an emotional need out there somewhere. Now I'll tell you who Jesus is, he's our Lord and Saviour. Now you see, everybody's happy. [Laughter and applause from audience, including a loud "Amen!"]

MONTGOMERY: I certainly hope that that goes into the transcript: both Professor

Fletcher's reply which was entirely ambiguous and the Amen which was equally ambiguous.

McCLURG: We have a question for Dr. Montgomery. Why must people be driven to the cross? What does this mean?

MONTGOMERY: This expression I used has to do with the need for forgiveness when a person violates the commands of God. When a person finds himself in an ambiguous ethical situation—and it should be noted that these ambiguous ethical situations are the product of the society that we ourselves create as fallen human beings —the individual is often at the point of violating a command of God, not because he wants to, but because he's damned if he does and damned if he doesn't. For example, one might have to shoot a sniper before he kills more people, as in the incident that happened at a university here in the States a few years ago. To kill a human being, if Jesus is right, is a sin. It's morally wrong. Human beings are not to be killed. Thou shalt not kill. In situations like this it may be necessary to judge the number of people who will be killed if the sniper remains alive and, under those circumstances, shoot the sniper. But such a decision doesn't morally vindicate the man who makes it. If the man is a Christian, this agonizing decision will cause him to look in the mirror and see himself as a member of a sinful society. His decision to shoot a fellow human being will compel him to seek forgiveness. Remember John Donne's great line: "Any mans death diminishes me, because I am involved in Mankinde; and therefore never send to know for whom the bell tolls; it tolls for thee." There is a solidarity in human life that requires a person to see his own culpability in situations like this and therefore to seek forgiveness. This is what I meant when I said, in quoting the New Testament, that the Law acts as a servant or slave to lead us to Christ:[1] our violations of God's perfect standards drive us to the place of forgiveness. The sad thing is that in so much of ethics—not merely situational ethics, but ethics in general— morality is so frequently employed as a device for getting us off the hook. What I want to stress is that *none* of us gets off the hook. If we once recognize this, then maybe we'll seek the help that we need. You can't force pills down people's gullets if they're convinced that they don't have any disease. One of the biggest dif-

---

[1] Gal. 3:24.

ficulties in our contemporary society is that we try to locate the evil in somebody else and then we try to get rid of him. The police are pigs or the students are worthless, and so on and so on. The Marxists are the devils or the Republicans are the devils or you name it. We try to isolate the evil and then get rid of it. But the teaching of the Bible is that we are thoroughly entrenched in this ourselves, so we can't toss rocks at someone else; we have to see the extent to which the moral ambiguities fall directly on us. We need forgiveness; and only when we receive it do we have our lives cleaned up so that we can start seeing situations accurately. [Applause.]

McCLURG: We have a question for Professor Fletcher. How do you derive the meaning "neighbor love" from the Greek word *agape*, which means divine love irrepective of faults, traits or characteristics of the one loved?

FLETCHER: Well, I derive the connotation neighbor love from the Greek *agapao* and the nominative form *agape* because that is the way in which it is ordinarily used, both in Hellenistic literature and in the Koine Greek of the New Testament. I don't know who sent this question, but

I think he needs to take another course in Greek. As a matter of fact, there are a great many different terms. But why should we get into this linguistic hassle about *storge, eros, philia,* and *agape*? Greek is an infinitely rich language, and the intention in the use of the term *agape,* beginning with the first translation in the Septuagint of the ancient Hebrew Scriptures, was precisely to make it perfectly clear to the people of the covenant that if they are to love in the sense in which we are, radically to love even the *enemy,* then we will not be selective and we will not be romantic. We will be comprehensive and inclusive, however painfully and difficultly, even to including the enemy himself. It is not essentially an emotional relationship or posture towards other people but a disposition of good will. [Applause.] I hadn't wanted to impose any theological sophistication tonight, but if that's what is wanted, let's do it!

McCLURG: A question for Dr. Montgomery. Dr. Montgomery states that one cannot believe what Professor Fletcher states due to Professor Fletcher's position that truth-telling is not an absolute. But whether or not one can believe another is a matter of trusting another even if one man claims he adheres to the truth always and the other man claims he does not always adhere to the truth. Is not the ability of the observer to believe either one a matter of trust?

MONTGOMERY: This is very well put. In the last analysis, of course, it's up to you people to determine whether or not what is said by anyone here is factually correct and an honest statement of views. That's definitely the case. Your responsibility as an audience is far greater than the responsibility of any of the speakers. Your job is to cogitate on all of this, work it through yourselves, and come to a decision. Presumably in university life we follow Socrates' axiom that the unexamined life is not worth living. What we're trying to do is to examine questions and come to conclusions on them. But the point that I was trying to make in my opening essay was this: the difference between Professor Fletcher and myself is not that under absolutely no circumstances does he tell the truth and under absolutely no circumstances would I lie! I think I've made it clear that there are ambiguous situations where I might have to lie. But for me, when I do this, it goes against my ethic. It is wrong; I know it's wrong; and it will cause me to get down on my knees and ask forgiveness for it. But in the case of Professor Fletcher, if he does this, it could be in *accord* with his ethic. There's a world of difference between these two positions.

FLETCHER: May I just make one comment on that last response? Again, you know, just something to salt away and worry about. Aren't you in effect telling us that in your ethics we are sometimes morally obliged to do what is wrong, and does that make any sense in terms of ethical analysis? [Applause from audience.]

MONTGOMERY: No, it obviously does not make any sense in terms of *your* ethical analysis, but that's what we are trying to determine—whether that ethical analysis is right.

FLETCHER: No. I'm trying, and you must correct me. I'm trying to get the import of what you're telling us about your ethical posture, and it appears to me that you are saying, "Yes, it is true that some of the time I might be morally obliged to do what is wrong." Is that what you're saying?

MONTGOMERY: What I'm saying is that it may be necessary to choose a lesser of evils. *But such a choice still remains an evil.*

FLETCHER: And isn't the logical import of the lesser-evil doctrine precisely that sometimes we might be morally obliged to do what is wrong?

MONTGOMERY: Well, this depends, of course, on what you mean by morally obliged. Certainly there is . . .

FLETCHER: I don't mean anything particularly subtle about it. [Applause.]

MONTGOMERY: No, but you must mean *something* by it, or you would not use the expression.

FLETCHER: All right.

MONTGOMERY: The point that I'm trying to make is that because something is a lesser evil doesn't somehow transmute it into a good. But that's what happens in situationalism. Lesser evils disappear from the class of evils; a person sticks in his thumb and pulls out a plum and is able to achieve moral vindication. I don't believe that this should be allowable within the framework of theological ethics.

FLETCHER: I think you did that better the first time!

MONTGOMERY: Yes, I do too! [Laughter.]

McCLURG: We have a question for Professor Fletcher. How can the individual person, with limited intelligence, know what will be the long-run consequences of the actions he takes in accordance with his situational judgment?

FLETCHER: Yes, I think very often we can see that this is one of the subtleties and difficulties of responsible decision making. Every responsible decision-maker in medicine, or public administration, or government, or anywhere else knows this. It's a difficult thing, indeed, always to realistically and adequately foresee not only the immediate but the remote consequences of this, that, or the other course of actions or policies that appear to be alternatives open to us. It is certainly true that children are inexperienced and unlearned, and there are many adults who are quite childish. But St. Paul made abundantly clear within the context of his own familiar antimony about law and grace that reliance upon law is essentially a neurotic maneuver. Because life is complicated and treacherous and difficult, people turn to arbitrary and rigid oversimplifications of life and

its richness, by too simply adopting rules
and by supposing that righteousness deon-
tologically consists in adherence to rules.
I just don't believe that this is psycho-
logically mature and I don't think it is
well grounded hermeneutically in the New
Testament. Life is much more risky than
that, and we can't comprehend everything
in rules. Little children often have to have
rules, and I suppose in a kind of paradoxical
way the situationist might very well say,
"Yes, of course, when law serves love's
purposes, use it and follow it." We do this
with children. We give them rules and in
a sense they need it for the sake of their
own security in a very puzzling world. But
we are also reassured that the children
are growing up when they cease to adhere
rigidly to rules and assume the burden
of conscience and make decisions as realistically as they know how, rather than
following prefabricated rules. However,
what's true of our psychometric develop-
ment I think carries a very important
message for ethical theory. Well—I won't
elaborate any more than that. [Applause.]

MONTGOMERY: Would you permit a
comment on that? Do we have time?
This question was a very good one; it's
the question that's been asked of utilitarian-

ism back to the days of Bentham and Mill,[1] namely: If your ethic is one of the greatest good for the greatest number, just how do you predict what will turn out to maximize good when you have no absolute principles? There was a thesis done not too long ago which speaks directly to this issue. Here are a few lines from it with an example:

> The impossibility of such ethical calculations can be demonstrated by reading Bentham who attempted to make moral decisions on the basis of mathematical calculations. Even the simplest ethical decision is impossible on such a basis. Suppose one is faced with the ethical decision of telling a lie to an employer. If he tells the truth, he suspects (who can know for sure!) he will be fired. If he is fired, what will the consequences be? He may find a better job and make more money, or he may find one that pays less. Can he predict how far he will be able to work his way up in each case? Perhaps he will be better off in the long run if he is fired. But what if he tells a lie and is not fired? Other questions must also be answered. If his lie is detected, will his fellow employees find out? How will they react? How will all related fac-

[1] Jeremy Bentham (1748-1832) and John Stuart Mill (1806-1873), the two leaders of the utilitarian movement in nineteenth century philosophical ethics.

tors balance out over an extended period of time? [1]

The utilitarians were a good deal more sophisticated in this than our present situationists, for they actually attempted to solve the problem by mathematical formulae— and the result was a complete mess! If you'd like to read the details of this dismal business, I'd suggest C. D. Broad's work, *Five Types of Ethical Theory,* in which analysis and critique are provided.[2] The fact of the matter is that you cannot predict with any degree of rigor in situations like this and therefore you find yourself where old Horatius Bonar said you would be: you are reduced to unprincipled action on the basis of some kind of last-minute mystic intuitions; moral action ironically grinds down to the very existential ethic that Professor Fletcher was condemning earlier. And as far as the "immaturity of rules," poor Jesus! He was obviously suffering from that kind of immaturity and evidently would like to have us suffer from it too.

[1] Erwin Wesley Lutzer, "A Reply to Joseph Fletcher" (unpublished M.A. Thesis, Chicago Graduate School of Theology, 1970), pp. 35-36.

[2] C. D. Broad, *Five Types of Ethical Theory* ("International Library of Psychology, Philosophy and Scientific Method"; London: Routledge and Kegan Paul, 1956), chap. vi ("Sidgwick"), pp. 246-52.

FLETCHER: I hope this academic community is equipped to see how tendentious this treatment of the problem of utilitarianism is! The suggestion is that the dozen eminent utilitarians in the contemporary philosophical scene are nitwits, you know, "Ha, ha, ridiculous, perfectly ridiculous." They may be wrong, you know, but in . . .

MONTGOMERY: I'm not saying that they're nitwits, but as a matter of fact, they're very few in number and . . .

FLETCHER: Why are you quoting C. D. Broad as the definitive discussant of the ethics and merits of utilitarianism?

MONTGOMERY: I'm not saying definitive; I'm saying suggestive. I think our audience would benefit from reading more on the subject, and they can work with a considerable amount of other material. They can, for example, do what I'm afraid you have not done in your works, namely, cover the history of the analytical criticism of ethics as presented by Kurt Baier, Stephen Toulmin, and so on! [1] These people have shown that the kind of attempt to

---

[1] Kurt Baier, *The Moral Point of View* (New York; Random House, 1965); Stephen Toulmin, *An Examination of the Place of Reason in Ethics* (Cambridge [Eng.]: Cambridge University Press, 1964).

build up an ethic from situations is bound to manifest the naturalistic fallacy.[1] You just end up with a description of what people are doing.

FLETCHER: Yes, but then on the other hand, you see, in their camp you get Robert Hare who disagrees with both Moore and Toulmin especially, and with Stevenson who is certainly on his own profession a neo-utilitarian.

MONTGOMERY: But all of them unite in agreeing that a situationalist ethic cannot rise above its situation.

McCLURG: Question for Dr. Montgomery. Is there such a thing as a boundary situation where a person must choose between two sins? If so, would not Christ have been subjected to such and thereby have sinned?

MONTGOMERY: The answer to the first half of this question is yes, very definitely, there are such boundary situations; but it doesn't follow that the answer to the second half is also yes. The latter depends entirely upon what situations Christ en-

---

[1] The "naturalistic fallacy"—an expression deriving from G. E. Moore's *Principia Ethica*, chap. i—refers to the confusion of "oughtness" (morals) with "isness" (mores).

countered, and, secondly, whether or not he suffered from a lack of knowledge of his total situation as we do. If he was subjected to our limitations of knowledge, then he would have found himself in the same kind of pickle that we find ourselves in. But the New Testament documents present Jesus not at all as—what was your expression?—a Jew of "little philosophical sophistication," but as very God of very God, who forgave sin, who got himself crucified on the charge of blasphemy, and who arose from the dead, vindicating his claim to Deity. A person like this was—in the words of the New Testament—"like us in all points and yet without sin." [1]

McCLURG: Question for Professor Fletcher: Does the cross event and subsequent resurrection have any purpose in your morality? If so, why? If you do not give the cross event and resurrection of Jesus Christ the utmost value or highest good, then what purpose or use is the life of Christ?

FLETCHER: I would say that I find in the Christ event and in the life and teachings of Jesus a paradigm or model of love and in terms of the Johannine propo-

_____
[1] Heb. 4:15.

sition *ho Theos agape estin* (God is love). This means that God *is* love, not that he gives it or offers it or intends it, but *is* it—in the indicative mood. I'd say that for me as a Christian situationist, the use (was that the phrase?) of Jesus, the value, purpose or use in the life of Christ was that he is the exemplar, he is the very model, he is the most. He is what I mean by love. There are many other things, you know, that can be said from a theological vantage point about Jesus in the terms of soteriology and what one's faith is about him with respect to man's destiny and salvation and so on, but in this context (the ethical one), I'd say that the most immediate bearing of the Jesus figure, if we may so express it, is that of paradigm, model, example . . . that's it.

McCLURG: Question for Dr. Montgomery. Are you addressing your audience as a Christian population or could your propositions apply to the world as a whole, i.e., to nations who do not accept the Ten Commandments or Jesus Christ?

MONTGOMERY: When the question says "the world as a whole," I suppose that it is spelled w-h-o-l-e.

McCLURG: Yes, that is c o r r e c t. [Laughter.]

MONTGOMERY I'm speaking as a Christian theologian here because we're dealing with what is presumably a theological ethic rather than a philosophical ethic. I think that Professor Fletcher's view boils down to a philosophical ethic, really a kind of glorified utilitarianism. But theoretically this is a theological problem and therefore I've spoken theologically. This means that some of what I've said would have little meaning to anybody who is not thinking in Christian terms, but the earlier remarks that I made in my formal presentation most definitely apply across the board. That is to say, in any society where truth-telling (for example) is not regarded as intrinsically good, a situation arises in which anything becomes possible. It is not a smear tactic or anything resembling it to cite the results in Soviet Russia of the principle that the end justifies the means. The fact of the matter is—and Russians themselves are seeing this—that kind of operation can bring about the collapse of a society. The purges that went on during the Stalinist era were perfectly hideous. This can happen anywhere in any kind of society where moral absolutes are jettisoned. If we consider the general world situation, therefore, we will confront societies which deteriorate in exact proportion to the decline of intrinsic moral values.

FLETCHER: I'd like to add a deviant comment about this very question. I think it is a smear tactic, Dr. Montgomery, to discuss the proposition that the end does in fact justify the means by citing the Commies. I spoke at the U.S. Air Force Academy about three weeks ago, near Colorado Springs, at their request, about conscience and military service. I took the position that what the U.S. Government is doing to the people in Southeast Asia is an example of a decision that the end justifies the means. They agreed with me without any question whatsoever. Why in the world should anybody suggest that it is only Soviet-power people who act on this presumably callous and ruthless theory? Everybody has to act on it. You yourself revealed that you do when you said that though abortion is wrong, sometimes you do it. Why? You can't possibly make any sense whatsoever out of your admission that we can sometimes kill tyrants, that we can sometimes terminate pregnancy, that we can sometimes tell lies, even though it is "wrong" to do it, except on the ground that in such tragic situations the end justifies the means. I don't know anything that presumably intelligent people talk more nonsense about than this perennial problem about the relationship between means and ends.

MONTGOMERY: Yes, and I think the maximum nonsense is the assertion that these are not inherently connected and that it's possible to separate them in such a way that one can employ any means in order to achieve an end.

FLETCHER: Who has said they're unconnected?

MONTGOMERY: That's the implication of the statement that only the end justifies the means.

FLETCHER: That is a logical implication of the proposition?

MONTGOMERY: Yes, because it then follows that you can employ any means, *any means,* that will reach the end which you desire.

FLETCHER: This is almost a classical example of an undistributed middle! [1]

MONTGOMERY: Well, in that case, will you please tell me what means are not justified?

_____
[1] Sic. The undistributed middle is a logical fallacy having the form:
Major premise:
 All A is B   All elephants have big ears.
Minor premise:
 All C is B   Socrates has big ears.
 (Conclusion)
 All C is A   Socrates is an elephant.

FLETCHER: What means are *not* justified?

MONTGOMERY: Yes.

FLETCHER: No means which leads to a malicious end is justified.

MONTGOMERY: In other words, the means . . .

FLETCHER: It's the end which determines whether the means will be employed. As a matter of fact, Lenin was quite right, you know, when in his *Philosophical Notebooks,* he said if the end doesn't justify the means, what in heaven's name does? An act which is, so to speak, employed meaninglessly without any kind of end is precisely irrational, it doesn't make sense. You know, I'm beginning to like you. You say so bluntly and plainly, "Yes, there are times when I would do things that I regard as wrong by nature." It's a beautiful example of what it means to say that the end justifies the means!

MONTGOMERY: Not at all, because this does not *justify* my act. It still turns out to be a wrong act. That's the gulf that separates us.

FLETCHER: Then you do agree that your theory, your ethics, calls upon you as a matter of obligation to do something that is wrong.

MONTGOMERY: In my ethic a lesser evil does not turn out to be a good by the fact that it's less evil than something else.

FLETCHER: Now we are getting circular.

MONTGOMERY: That is *not* circular; it's *the point!*

FLETCHER: I . mean our discussion is getting circular.

MONTGOMERY: And as to my use of Lenin and company, I think I made it very clear that I. don't regard evil as attaching to one particular culture or to one particular philosophy of life. I would certainly be willing to agree that the U.S. has provided hideous examples of the end justifying the means. As a matter of fact, I cited Lenin because *you* employ him as *your* example in your chapter on the end as sole justification for the means.[1]

FLETCHER: All right, thank you, that's fine, thank you very much. That's good. [Laughter from audience.]

------

[1] Fletcher, SITUATION ETHICS.

McCLURG: A question for Professor Fletcher. You use the term 'Christian' repeatedly. How do you define the term Christian? More accurately, what are the requirements necessary for an individual to be classified as a Christian?

FLETCHER: That question, if fully and adequately responded to, would entail quite an agenda with alas quite a spectrum of opinion. Such opinions are faith affirmations, not empirically verifiable or justifiable. I don't want to oversimplify it, but it strikes me, off the cuff, that the essence of a good answer would be that a Christian is one who calls Jesus Lord.

MONTGOMERY: You m e a n: accepts Jesus as Lord even when he seems to want us to hold things as intrinsically good— even when he wants us to follow an absolute moral law?

FLETCHER: Good. Sure. [Laughter.]

MONTGOMERY: Just curious.

FLETCHER: Or, to put it a little bit more carefully, accept Jesus as Lord even though to *some* of those who call him Lord he seemed to be saying that we should absolutize or idolatrize some normative principles.

McCLURG: A question for Dr. Montgomery. By our knowledge of "absolute values," is a detailed application always exhaustively specified? If not, wouldn't omniscience be required on the part of each moral agent as he applies "absolutes" to specific situations? Without it, the absolute will no longer be absolute as applied!

MONTGOMERY: Dear me. The principles of absolute or intrinsic Christian morality are certainly not exhaustive or exhausting. They don't cover all conceivable particular situations in the sense of offering a rule book in which you check the index under whatever problem you have and obtain a rule which is exactly coterminus with the problem. But that doesn't mean that the principles that *are* given are not intrinsically valid. That is to say, even though the Ten Commandments don't deal with all of the particular ambiguous moral situations that Professor Fletcher cites, they must be brought to bear where they *do* have reference. We must not jump from the true fact that the biblical material doesn't give us the sort of thing that Rabbinic teaching did—x-number of rules for every conceivable situation—to the false conclusion that the principles which *are* revealed are therefore not valid. Agreed:

the application of biblical commands does have to be made by finite individuals and the application is often a matter of agonizing conscience. But the question is whether you'd be better off with no absolute principles at all! I think we've already seen what some of the results of that can be.

FLETCHER: I didn't know anybody up here was arguing for the antinomian position.

MONTGOMERY: By the antinomian position, Professor Fletcher refers to the viewpoint that accepts no laws whatsoever —even as relativistic guidelines. I'm not speaking of that. But if one reduces moral principles to a take-it-or-leave-it basis according to the situation, it seems to me that the result is not at all, as you claim, a happy medium between legalism and antinomianism. In point of fact, I'm convinced—and many of your other critics have pointed this out as well—that your three categories of legalism, antinomianism, and situationism are a kind of a Procrustean bed. One doesn't have to choose among these in the sense in which you've described them.

McCLURG: We have time for one more question for each of the debaters. Question for Professor Fletcher. In situational ethics, what authority does the Bible have?

FLETCHER: None, unless the situationist is a Christian. Recently in New Haven Ayn Rand, who as you know is the barnyard philosopher of a thing called Objectivism, a straight egoistic ethics, presented her thesis. Then I presented mine and the chairman asked us to exchange a bit as we've done here before it was thrown out to the floor. Her first question to me was, "Are you trying to tell me that we ought to love everybody?" When I said, "Yes, precisely," she said, "Well, that's the ethics of a whore." There we were in that semantic swamp about what is to be connoted by the term "love" and when I struggled a bit with this, she got the point readily enough (she was an intelligent person) and said, "All right then, instead of whore put dope." She's not a Christian, but she is a situationist and she doesn't take any of her normative principles as things that are to be followed instead of her conscience, regardless of relativities of circumstances. But she's serving an altogether different *summum bonum* or first order of good than you and I would. One becomes a Christian on grounds other than ethical, in my opinion, but when one *is* a Christian and has made the faith affirmation that Jesus is Lord, he then turns around and looks at his ethics and reexamines and reconstructs his ethics in the light of that confession.

McCLURG: We have a final question for Dr. Montgomery. I realize that you are not a Catholic, but what of the Roman Catholic doctrine of just and unjust wars? Generally speaking, is it not true that most Christian faiths follow that doctrine? But is not this a case of situation ethics? If situation ethics is wrong, is not all killing wrong?

MONTGOMERY: It's always a little awkward to get a confessional question like this—particularly at the end of our discussion. Doubtless most of you people know that I am a Lutheran and so this makes the thing a little bit sticky. To be frank, I'm not entirely happy with the just war concept as it is presented by the casuistical tradition within Roman Catholicism. I think that many Roman Catholics are likewise beginning to question this. There is a sense—and it's Professor Fletcher's sense —in which a war might be "just," that it might hopefully result in less hideousness than not fighting. But I want to stress as strongly as I possibly can that in terms of the biblical ethic and the classical Christian faith, Protestant and Catholic, no war is inherently just. Wars are *damnable*. The consequences of them for the people involved, whether the victors or the defeated, are just too awful to describe. I think we make a very great mistake if we try to slither ethically around this question. Now, again, this doesn't mean that the Christian may not find himself in a position where he cannot help but fight. But heaven help him if he thereby feels that he is engaged in a justifiable activity. He is in fact participating in the kind of activity that we sinful and fallen human beings have brought about on this planet, and we had better come to see that this situation is a good deal more wretched than we are usually willing to admit. Hopefully, we have finally gone beyond that nineteenth-century confidence in ourselves expressed by the early twentieth-century adage of the French psychologist Coué: "Every day in every way we're getting better and better." I hope we're beginning to see that what we have really become is more efficiently nasty toward one another, and that this points up our most fundamental human need. Perhaps ethics doesn't necessarily drive a person to religious commitment, but I guess that one of the most basic points I'm trying to make is that ethics *ought to do so.* If you honestly look at the fallen world and yourself, I wonder if you aren't driven to a different kind of evaluation of your relation to the universe than you had before. I wonder if perhaps you may not find yourself driven to Jesus Christ.

McCLURG: On behalf of the Cultural Arts Board of San Diego State College, I would like to thank both our debaters, Professor Fletcher and Dr. Montgomery, for a most stimulating evening.